Inspirational Readings for the Christian Woman

Carolyn Baldwin Tucker, Ph.D.

D0916631

Published by 21st Century Christian

ISBN-13: 978-0-89098-540-3

eISBN: 978-0-89098-956-2

21st Century Christian Bookstore
P. O. Box 40526
2809 12th Avenue South
Nashville, TN 37204

Printed in the United States of America

Unless otherwise indicated, all scriptures are quoted from the King James Version.

Cover design by Jonathan Edelhuber.

Contents

FOREWARD

Inspirational Readings for the Christian Woman is composed of various presentations that I have given over the years and lessons that I have taught in the Ladies Sunday Morning Bible Class. This book is geared primarily toward women, and contains twenty-seven short readings that are spiritually oriented and scripturally based. The readings are grouped according to central themes. It is my prayer that this book will serve as encouragement to the readers and their understanding of the scriptures, while strengthening their walk with Christ.

Carolyn Baldwin Tucker

Acknowledgements and Dedication

First and foremost, I want to give praise, glory, and honor to God who is the center of my life "the giver of every good and perfect gift;" to His son, and my Saviour, Jesus Christ, who gave His life that I might have "life and have it more abundantly" and to the Spirit of God that dwells within me and guides me along my Christian journey.

This book is dedicated to my parents, the late Mr. George Edgar and Mrs. Susie Mae Baldwin, whose love and commitment to the Lord led me in the path of righteousness, laying the foundation upon which my faith would grow and develop.

Expressions of deepest love and appreciation are given to:

- My husband of forty-two years, Jesse Frank Tucker, my best friend, who has been my continued source of support and encouragement.
- My daughter Susan Tucker Jones (an attorney), and my son Randall Fouse Tucker, Sr. (a Gospel Preacher) for becoming the young Christian adults that are "crowns of glory" to a mother's head, and Ericca Thompson Tucker (my daughter–in-law) for being "a help meet" for my son.
- My grandchildren, who I trust will become faithful, dedicated Christians advancing the cause of Christ.
- My sister Mrs. Jewell Baldwin Cousin, who lovingly

reared me after the passing of our parents (George and Susie Baldwin).

- My other siblings, their spouses, and their children: James (Lorene) Baldwin, Sr.; Evelyn D. Baldwin Johnson; John (Ruby) Baldwin, Sr.; Irene (Morris) Baldwin Chapman; Marion E. Baldwin and Gilbert (Janice) Baldwin, Sr. for your encouragement and support.
- My mother-in-law Mrs. L. Josephine Tucker for being a good Christian mother to my husband and his siblings.

In addition, I hope that this book will provide insight and encouragement to anyone who reads it and cause each reader to continue in the study of God's Word.

"To God Be The Glory"

Jesus

A Focus on Jesus

Philippians 2:10 — "That at the name of Jesus every knee should bow, of the things in heaven, and things in earth, and things under the earth."

It is important for Christian women to remain focused on Jesus, even though the devil sends all kinds of distractions to cause us to lose focus. We must rebuke the devil and hold fast to Christ. When problems arise on the job, or in the home, many times we forget the ONE to whom we should turn. We often forget that Jesus is the "burden bearer," "the solid rock," "the refuge in time of trouble." Sometimes we become so overwhelmed with the circumstances that surround us, we forget the One who can deliver us from all problems, hurt and harm. In the midst of all of the storms of life, in the face of adversity and problems, we must stay focused on Jesus in order to be at peace on this earth and make heaven our home.

The name of Jesus is powerful and worthy to be praised. The name of Jesus is to be exalted above all names by those who believe that He is the "Christ the Son of the living God" (Matthew 16:16). When we read Acts 4:12, we can clearly understand the importance of the name of Jesus, "…for there is none other name under heaven given among men, whereby we must be saved."

As Christian women, we must stay focused on the fact that Jesus is "the first and the last, the beginning and the end, the Alpha and Omega." If we believe that He is the Christ, we will have no problem proclaiming His name and submitting to His will. Our talk will reflect that we know Jesus. Our actions will reflect that we are walking with the Savior and that HE is the center of our lives. If we stand for Christ now, He will stand for us in the judgment. He will take our burdens and make them HIS.

Being a Christian is not easy and it was never promised to be easy. We are told in 2 Timothy 3:12 "Yea, and all that will live godly in Christ Jesus shall suffer persecution." Even when faced with problems that are not of our own making, we should hold fast to the Lord, trusting in His Word and expecting a deliverance from the situation. We must rest on the scripture that says, "…no good thing will he withhold from them that walk uprightly" (Psalm 84:11). If there is something that we want and we are denied that request, as Christians, we must believe that it was not the will of God for the request to be granted because He could be saving us from something or saving us for something else. Still our faith must be grounded and rooted in the Lord.

Christian women must remember that our purpose for being here is to (1) prepare us to live eternally with God (2) try to influence others to live a Christian life and (3) be examples to the world. Remaining focused on Christ and doing His will, ensures that we can be with HIM in eternity. Though the world is unfocused and yields to the many distractions of life, Christian women must remain focused on the true source of life and power – Jesus Christ.

Thought Questions:

1. Do you sometimes feel alone although others are around you?
2. When this happens, do you think about how Jesus may have felt on the cross?
3. Have you ever sat down and really counted your blessings?

Jesus – The Great Burden Bearer

Matthew 11:28-30 — "Come unto me, all ye that labour and are heavy laden, and I will give you rest. Take my yoke upon you, and learn of me; for I am meek and lowly in heart: and ye shall find rest unto your souls. For my yoke is easy, and my burden is light."

In dealing with the struggles of this life and the many problems that beset us, as Christians we should take comfort in knowing that "we do not bear our burdens alone." Problems that arise in relationships between friends or loved ones can be eased through a reliance on Jesus who is Lord. Our trust often times is mislaid when we place it in man. We may become dismayed by the behavior of those that we have trusted. Our faith, hope and trust should rest solely in the ONE who has never forsaken us, and who will never forsake us.

Trying to carry the weight of families and responsibilities of jobs can cause women to become disheartened. When we rely on our own abilities and strength, we soon find out that we are weak and not able to sustain. Drawing on the strength of the Lord opens up a whole new reservoir of energy, resilience and sustenance. Jesus has unlimited amounts of power to hold us up when we, of our own strength, begin to sink. Burdens become easier when we know we do not carry them alone.

Problems that we face in relationships often are harder to endure than problems of finances, and those that are job related. Working through the difficulties of misunderstandings can be a hard task. When friends betray you, know that the Lord is still in control and He will fortify you in your time of dismay. Jesus is an "everlasting friend" who will take your problems, own them and resolve them. JESUS **IS** THE GREAT BURDEN BEARER.

There is no need for us to carry our burdens alone. Jesus, who is our "everlasting friend," has offered us assistance, peace and rest. Jesus knows our limitations and "he knows how much we can bear." He knows all about us and is willing to be our source of comfort and strength. He will never betray us and will support us when no one else does. He will be with us always. From the beginning of time—there was Jesus; throughout time—there is Jesus; and when time shall be no more—there will be Jesus. From the beginning to the ending—there is Jesus.

Thought Questions:

1. When facing problems do you ever feel overwhelmed?
2. Do you turn to the Word to receive comfort from the Lord?
3. Do you know that there are women in the Bible who faced many problems and received comfort through the words of Jesus?

The Redemptive Blood of Jesus

Romans 3:24-25 — "Being justified freely by his grace through the redemption that is in Christ Jesus: Whom God hath set forth to be a propitiation through faith in his blood, to declare his righteousness for the remission of sins that are past, through the forbearance of God."

We are blessed because we serve a righteous and forgiving God who was willing to sacrifice His only begotten Son to save sinners who rejected Him. God's love is so encompassing and forgiving that He does not want any of us to be lost. To insure that we are afforded the opportunity to live with Him in heaven, He sent His Son to shed His blood on the cross so that we could be saved.

When studying the redemptive saving power of Jesus' blood there are three terms that we need to consider. Those are "atonement", "propitiation", and "reconciliation". All of those words have to do with God's unending love for us and His desire for us to be restored to Him in spite of our desire to sin. God sent the perfect one, His Son—Jesus, to earth to be born of a woman, suffer on the cross, bearing the burden of our sins as an atonement for our iniquity; and then to rise from the grave and ascend to heaven (Matthew 1:21; Ephesians 1:7). By doing so, He became our propitiation in calming God's wrath towards us because of our sins. God allowed His "only begotten Son" to die for our sins so that we could be reconciled back to Him. Christ is our reconciliation back to God.

7

Life comes from God. Blood is the life source for man. Of all the things that man can make, he cannot make blood. The shedding of Jesus blood now allows us to enter into heaven by being baptized in the water and blood of the Lamb. The blood of Jesus cleanses us from sin, puts us in position for being saved in the end and gives us eternal life (1 John 1:7).

As Christian ladies, we have a responsibility to try to pattern our lives so that young girls can see Christ in us. Our lives must demonstrate that we value our salvation and the sacrifice that Jesus made for us to receive eternal life. When we think about how Christ shed His blood on the cross so that we would not have to suffer, we should lay aside all of our malice, evil thoughts, and other negativity. We should then reflect on His suffering, pain and agony. When we do this, we begin to appreciate and understand the importance of the saving power of Jesus' precious blood.

Our redemption is by the life blood of the spotless Lamb of God. We should rejoice each day knowing that we have the promise of glory; to be forever in the presence of Jesus if we live according to His commandments. Our rejoicing should be never ending because we know that God's love is never ending.

Thought Questions:

1. Why is the blood of Christ essential to our salvation?
2. Why would God want to redeem man?
3. What does propitiation mean?

The Saving Power of Jesus' Blood

Revelation 1:5 — "And from Jesus Christ, who is the faithful witness, and the first begotten of the dead, and the prince of the kings of the earth. Unto him that loved us, and washed us from our sins in his own blood."

When Jesus died on the cross, shedding His blood, it was an unprecedented sign of the perfect life being sacrificed for man to be released from sin and be reconciled back to God. Because of the shedding of Jesus' blood, we are able to be forgiven of our sins over and over and over again. This forgiveness of our sins allows us to escape the "second death"—that eternal death. For those who put on Jesus in the "watery grave of baptism," there is hope for eternal life with Jesus our Savior and God our Father.

The blood of Jesus acts as a cleansing agent for our sins. "…though your sins be as scarlet, they shall be as white as snow; though they be red like crimson, they shall be as wool" (Isaiah 1:18). Blood is the source of life for the physical body and Jesus' blood is the life source for the spiritual body. If we live according to the commandments of Jesus, we will have the gift of eternal life.

By Jesus shedding His blood, we are able to become a part of His kingdom. He broke down the partition between Jews and Gentiles. By His death and resurrection the old covenant was ended and the new covenant was begun. That covenant is of "grace and truth." The blood of Jesus shields us from punishment for sin because through baptism our sins are washed away. His death involved the shedding of blood and the blood that began saving two thousand years ago, continues to save today. Jesus' blood provides the protection that we need to see us through problems and adversities of this world.

As Christians, we should be willing to share the good news of Jesus and the saving power of His blood. Those around us should know that we are Christians not because we tell them, but because we show them. We are the redeemed and should be living as the redeemed.

Thought Questions:

1. Have you ever envisioned the pain and agony of Jesus on the cross?
2. Have you ever (by actions or speech) denied that you are a Christian?
3. Did you know that when you live in sin, you crucify Christ again?

Jesus - The Light of The World

John 12:35-36 — "Then Jesus said unto them, Yet a little while is the light with you. Walk while ye have the light, lest darkness come upon you: for he that walketh in darkness knoweth not whither he goeth. While ye have light, believe in the light, that ye may be the children of light."

Jesus is and has always been the source of light, the "well-spring of wisdom and the pathway to righteousness." Coming to an understanding of His Word allows us to know good from evil, right from wrong. For those who abide in the Word and follow the Word, Jesus provides the guidance that is needed to help us maneuver through the pitfalls of this life. For "[t]hy word is a lamp unto my feet, and a light unto my path"(Psalm 119:105).

Today, we have the written Word to guide us, when Jesus walked this earth, those who were blessed to see Him and be with Him had the "living word" present with them and "many received him not." Belief on Jesus offers the Christian a world of light and understanding. The one who believes on Jesus and follows His commandments, will find insight into life's perplexing problems. A study of His Word, an openness of the mind to receive the Word, and a commitment by the Christian to do those things presented in the Word, will cause that person to "see with new eyes and to hear with open ears."

Light is known for providing a means by which people see. Having light prevents us from bumping into things, losing our balance, and falling. However, when we refuse to see Jesus, He sometimes has to let us fall and be knocked down before we can see what we need to do. Jesus, who is our light, allows us to see situations from a different perspective. Jesus puts balance into our lives and keeps us from falling into the pitfalls of life. We must however, read the word in order to have the source of light to guide us. Reading of the words of Jesus is refreshing and can lift us when feeling depressed, guide us in our decisions and keep us from doing things that will cause us problems later.

Light and darkness cannot exist in the same place. When light comes in, darkness moves out. Jesus is light and the devil is darkness. "Where Jesus abides, the devil cannot find a resting place."

Thought Questions:

1. Do you believe that the Bible has answers to the problems of today?
2. Do you see your Bible as a guide to your daily living?
3. Have you ever read the entire book of Proverbs?

Guided by the Spirit

Christian Women Walking in the Spirit

Ephesians 6:11 — "Put on the whole armor of God, that ye may be able to stand against the wiles of the devil."

Christian women can become fortified through a diligent study of the Word in order to be prepared to walk in the spirit while doing "battle with the devil." We are living in a world that is full of treachery and deceit which is often made manifest through the actions of those with whom we have contact. The Christian woman must be diligent in her study of the Word so that she will be able to use the Word in answer to the call of the world. The answer that is used so well in the scriptures is the one that Jesus used, "it is written." In order for us to know what is written we must read the Word and be prepared to do battle with the devil by using the Word as our defense. The Word strengthens us as we read it and the Holy Spirit guides us in our understanding.

A major element in "fighting against the wiles of the devil" is knowing what is written and where to find what is written. It is important to have a working knowledge of the Bible in order to "be ready to give an answer to the hope that lies within you." When people commit evil acts toward one another, it is the devil at work; even working in places where you would think not. The scriptures tell us that there is "spiritual wickedness in high places." By knowing this, we should not be surprised when we hear of persons in authority or those with great responsibility becoming involved with unrighteous activities.

Christians must be adept in recognizing the "wiles" of the devil as being the trickery that he has people to do to deceive others. The "games people play" with each other that are unkind are examples of the tricks of the devil. The devil and his servants are masters in the art of deception.

The best way for Christian women to deal with the problems of this world is to be fully clothed in the Word of God with knowledge of the promises of God. The Word of God is the sword of the Spirit and must be a part of the armor and defense. The Bible tells us to stand—not sit—but stand. Stand ready for battle: Standing strong in the faith and "in the power of his Word." Walking in the Spirit means that we are in step with the Spirit and He is central to our lives.

Walking in the spirit means that we are focused on the Lord and minding His Word through concentration on good thoughts. The Christian woman seeks to demonstrate the fruit of the Spirit in her daily walk. Persons who come in contact with the Christian woman should know that she is a Christian by her talk, behavior and the company that she keeps.

Thought Questions:

1. Do you find that when you have not studied the Word, it is harder to withstand the pressures of the day?
2. Have you tried to memorize passages in the Bible?
3. How do you think you can improve your walk in the Spirit?

The Christian Woman Praying in the Spirit of Hope

Psalm 121:1 — "I will lift up mine eyes to the hills from whence cometh my help."

The Christian woman who prays in the Spirit is a powerful force with which to reckon. She understands that prayer is the method by which we, as Christians, make our requests known to God. Prayer affords us the opportunity to communicate with the ONE who controls time, destiny, and all other forces.

Prayer is the most powerful vehicle available to the Christian woman. Prayer allows us to request from God the release of that portion of HIS power which we need in order to endure. God wants us to pray to Him while being in submission to His will. Isaiah 65:24 says that God "before they call, [God] will answer; and while they are yet speaking, [He] will hear." God knows our thoughts even before we think them.

Jesus tells us that "all things, whatsoever ye shall ask in prayer, believing, ye shall receive" (Matthew 21:22). We must have the faith to believe that it will come to pass. We find in the gospels many references that Jesus made to prayer where He tells us that if we abide in Him and His Word abides in us, we can receive whatever we desire and ask in prayer.

The Christian woman who prays in the spirit of hope

16

channels out all of life's distractions and focuses on the power of God. The one who seeks the assistance of God through prayer is using the conduit by which the spiritual realm becomes a part of our natural lives. Our spirits require the presence of God for renewal and strengthening. When we pray in the Spirit we are feeding our souls the nourishment needed to be sustained.

Prayer acts as the oxygen passage for our spiritual beings. We have to keep our physical air passage clear and the same is true for our spiritual air passage. This is done through prayer and supplication to our heavenly Father. We sometimes become so concerned with the problems of life that we forget to pray the prayer of faith—knowing that we will receive if we ask believing.

When praying in the Spirit, we are assisted by the Holy Spirit in making our requests known to God. Through intercession of the "groanings" of the Holy Spirit, our requests are carried to God and "laid at his feet."

A tree that is disconnected from its roots cannot survive. In like manner, our spirit, when disconnected from HIS Spirit, cannot long endure.

Thought Questions:

1. How often do you pray?
2. Do you have a specific time of day when you talk with God?
3. How can you improve your prayer life?

The Fruit of the Spirit

Galatians 5:22-23 — "But the fruit of the Spirit is love, joy, peace, longsuffering, gentleness, goodness, faith, meekness, temperance: against such there is no law."

We have read, heard, known and studied the scripture that tells us "God is a Spirit: and they that worship him must worship him in spirit and in truth" (John 4:24). This scripture presents the concept that God receives worship that is done in spirit and in truth. Our worship to God must be sincere and in love. The things that we do in serving the Lord should be a testimony to the fact that we are His and that we bear the fruit of His Spirit.

The fruit of the Spirit will be seen by the manner in which we treat our fellow man. Jesus said while here on earth "... the tree is known by his fruit" (Matthew 12:33). If we bear envying, hatred and strife; our fruit is not of the Spirit. If we bear the kind of traits listed in Galatians 5:22-23, we are exemplifying the characteristics that God would have us exemplify. The fruit that is seen outside is a reflection of what is actually inside. An orange tree cannot bear apples, nor can an apple tree bear oranges. The fruit that we see on the tree lets us know what kind of tree it is. If we have kindness, goodness, love, faith and other spiritual fruit seen by the deeds that we do, we are then demonstrating the fruit of the Spirit.

Demonstrating the fruit of the Spirit is not an easy task. When some people know that you are trying to live a Christian life, they become centered on witnessing your downfall. When you are kind to some individuals, they return evil for your good. Others are determined to make your life miserable. Do not be overcome by their evil actions. Know that people who do such are not happy with themselves and they are not the children of God.

Do not treat others as they are—treat others as you want them to become. While it will not be easy to do, it is important to not allow others to steal your joy. Do not allow others to control your actions by what they do. While we may not be able to change other people, we can always change ourselves and how we respond to them. Generally, when we change our behavior, others cannot continue to respond in the way they have always responded. So the best way to control the behavior of others is to control our own behavior. We should ask ourselves in certain situations "What would Jesus have me to do?" By allowing Jesus to be the center of our lives, we take the focus off of us and we can then focus on Jesus and what he would have us to do. God is love and if we are to be like Him, we must demonstrate love —one of the most important fruits of the Spirit.

Thought Questions:

1. Are there some people that you find difficult to love?
2. What are you doing to overcome the barrier(s) to love?
3. How can you condition yourself to move around the barrier(s)?

Spirit Ordered Steps

Psalm 119:133 — "Order my steps in thy word: and let not any iniquity have dominion over me."

In order for the Christian woman to be in step with the Spirit, she must walk in the Spirit as walking according to the teachings of the Bible. The places that she goes should be places that she would feel comfortable in if she knew the Lord might meet her there. As we take our daily walks, interacting with others and going about our tasks, do we ever think: Am I doing what Jesus would have me do?

Psalm 119:133 is a request to the Lord by the Psalmist to not only "order my steps in thy word," but to "let not any iniquity have dominion over me." The Psalmist is requesting the Lord to channel his walk in the understanding of the Word so that he will be able to keep sin and evilness from overtaking him. The study of the Word of God fortifies the individual to be able to withstand negative forces that are ever so present in today's world. Things that could have "dominion" over people could be their love for taking strong drink; seeing certain kinds of movies; playing cards; skirting the truth and/or smoking. Those are only a few examples of things that could overtake a person. Any thing that a person does which she cannot control, and is allowed to go unchecked, will probably eventually have "dominion" over her.

As we look closely at the verse, we can know that the Psalmist is asking for direction and guidance in his walk or journey while here on earth. That walk also, in today's world includes our talk and interactions that we have with others. It could be stated that the Psalmist asks the Lord to direct him in the study of the Word in terms of how he should proceed in life. The Word is a guide and road map from earth to heaven.

Psalm 119 is a plea to God for knowledge of the Word and protection against those who might do harm. The Psalmist does not want to go in the presence of those that are evil and he is aware that association with those who do wrong might influence him. Therefore, he pleads with the Lord to let him know His commandments and to keep them very close to him. The Psalmist is wanting to do the Will of God.

Christian women must be mindful of where we go and the environment in which we find ourselves. In large measure, this will determine how strong we will remain in the keeping of Jesus' commandments. It is important for Christians to associate with other Christians so that those of like minds will strengthen one another.

Thought Questions:

1. Do you study to increase your understanding of what "thus sayeth the Lord"?
2. Have you made a commitment to following the commandments of Christ?
3. Do you allow others to prevent you from doing the will of God?

A Wise Woman

A Wise Christian Woman

Proverbs 14:1 — "Every wise woman buildeth her house: but the foolish plucketh it down with her hands."

The Christian woman should be a wise woman who builds her house on sound principles. She works diligently to insure that she minds the affairs of her household in a Godly manner. She works to strengthen those who are in her house and she does so in a loving and giving manner. The wise Christian woman models the kind of example her children can follow.

The wise woman avoids situations that give rise to confusion and works to maintain harmony in the home. She is one who puts herself last so that others in the home are attended. She finds ways to assist others in her household and is faithful to those around her. She teaches her children self-discipline and works to build character in her children.

In building her house the Christian woman seeks the security of a personal relationship with Christ. The wise woman is centered on Christ; following His doctrine and commandments. She is conservative in her spending habits and does not demand the latest furniture nor the most up-to-date clothing. She looks for ways that she can cut expenses and uses her resources wisely. She establishes a budget and adheres to that budget, being a good steward of the blessings which have been entrusted to her. She knows she is not a "fashion queen" and that does not bother her because she knows that God does not look on the outer appearance but "at the heart."

On the other hand, the foolish woman buys everything that she desires. She does not care if she causes her family hardship because everyone else's needs are secondary to hers. She acts in a manner that will cause others to dislike, distrust and disrespect her. She does not hold to truth and speaks words that are hateful and toxic. She seeks to advance her cause at the expense of others. Her focus is not on maintaining her home in an appropriate manner; rather it is on uplifting herself and her prideful ways.

The wise Christian woman is kind to others and is not malicious or envying in her deeds. She does not harbor malice nor ill-will toward others. She is not spiteful or envious and does not plot for revenge. The wise Christian woman exhibits Christ in her life and serves as a living epistle to the glory and power of God. In her business affairs she demonstrates forthrightness and honesty. She is respected by her peers and speaks the truth.

Thought Questions:

1. Are you a wise Christian woman?
2. Do you make decisions based on sound thinking and Christian principles?
3. Are you teaching wise practices to younger women?

The Christian Woman Seeking Wisdom

Proverbs 3:13-14 — "Happy is the man that findeth wisdom, and the man that getteth understanding. For the merchandise of it is better than the merchandise of silver, and the gain thereof than fine gold."

These verses emphasize the importance of wisdom and understanding as being more precious than the worth of silver and gold. Wisdom allows one to know what to do with the blessings of wealth and riches. For the person who has obtained wealth and does not have wisdom to properly utilize the wealth, it can become of no benefit to the person.

Wisdom allows one to understand the various responsibilities associated with blessings and resources. It allows a person to know how to use those resources in ways that will not only benefit the individual but will also have positive impact on others.

The understanding that accompanies wisdom causes an individual to think about the positive aspects and the negative aspects of situations. It assists the person in knowing how best to use resources and refrain from ventures that will produce negative results.

People who are not wise in their wealth soon find themselves in a worse state after having received wealth than before they obtained it. Those who lack wisdom and are blessed with high paying jobs many times will not spend their income wisely and overspend their finances. Events such as this result in foreclosures and loss of property, and will also cause other family problems.

Knowledge is good to have but wisdom and understanding in applying the knowledge are to be valued more. Proper application of the knowledge, through wisdom, will yield far greater results than merely having knowledge. Wisdom in the daily exercise of our affairs will cause us to think long term before hastily acting on impulse. Wisdom should rule in the lives of Christians.

James 1:5 tells us "If any of you lack wisdom, let him ask of God, that giveth to all men liberally, and upbraideth not; and it shall be given him." Not only is wisdom good for managing one's business but it is profitable for basic living. For the Christian woman who desires wisdom, it is important to know that God is the source of wisdom. Seeking to do the will of God and asking Him for wisdom will provide the Christian woman with essentials necessary for strong spiritual living.

Thought Questions:

1. Do you feel that you are wise?
2. Have you asked God to increase your wisdom?
3. How has your wisdom benefited others?

Truth and the Wise Woman

1 Samuel 12:24 — "Only fear the LORD, and serve him in truth with all your heart: for consider how great things he hath done for you."

The wise woman builds her house on the truth of God. She works diligently to be sure that her words, her works and her thoughts are grounded in truth and righteousness. She patterns her life after the qualities of Jesus. She is a Christian and, therefore, her behavior is "Christ like." She builds her house on the solid foundation. She builds her house on the truth of God. Deuteronomy 32:4 says, "He is the Rock, his work is perfect: for all his ways are judgment: a God of truth and without iniquity, just and right is he."

In building her house on truth, the wise woman knows that she must not pretend to be something that she is not. She refuses to be hypocritical in her dealings with others because she knows that hypocrisy is not godly. She also knows that in order to inherit eternal life she must be true and faithful, not deceiving others by her actions. The wise woman knows that her children are watching, taking note and modeling the kind of example that she sets forth.

The wise Christian woman knows that truth will prevail even though it appears to be hidden. She teaches her children to trust in the Lord and establishes truth as a measure for living. She does not show partiality and treats all persons with respect and dignity (1 Timothy 5:21). She knows that her life and actions must be built on truth and that a demonstration of her faith is a testimony to the manner in which truth is a part of her life. She knows and holds fast to the concept that in order to see Jesus, she must base her life on Jesus who is the "truth" (John 14:6).

Telling the truth frees us of the hassle of trying to remember what we have said. This is because the truth never changes. Lies are built on lies and must continue to be told to try to keep one from being caught in a lie. This however, is dangerous because truth will prevail even though lies have been told. Ultimately, truth will win out over lies and will free the person of the burden of sin. Jesus said, "Ye shall know the truth, and the truth shall make you free" (John 8:32).

Thought Questions:

1. Have you ever observed the behaviors and speech of persons who do not value the truth?
2. Have you ever believed someone was telling you the truth only to later learn she was being untruthful?
3. How can the Christian help the person who seems to have a problem with telling the truth?

Humility and the Christian Woman's Home

Proverbs 22:4 — "By humility and the fear of the LORD, are riches, and honour, and life."

A wise woman knows the importance of humility being demonstrated in the home. She will encourage those in her household to be of an humble spirit and one that is contrite. She provides the atmosphere that will encourage humility in the rearing of her children. Being boastful and proud are traits that she avoids. The wise Christian woman knows if she is humble in spirit, fearing the Lord and obeying His commandments, blessings and honor will be bestowed upon her household.

A wise Christian woman considers others before herself. She exercises faith in the Word of God and humbly submits herself to the instruction of the Lord. By doing so, her wisdom increases as she seeks to do the will of the Lord. When people give her compliments, she will not become arrogant or high minded. She accepts those compliments and reflects them back to the Lord.

In today's society, people are quick to talk about their accomplishments, abilities and awards. Humility is not often demonstrated as individuals interact with one another. It almost appears that each person must have a greater story to tell than the other person. It demonstrates the competitiveness that is in the world and the manner in which the devil divides us – even those in the church.

The Christian woman needs to be sound in her belief system; knowing that it is not by her power that things are accomplished but by the power of the Spirit that works within her. She should be not so engrossed with being recognized that she forgets to be grateful for the talents that she possesses which come as a result of the grace of God and not of her own making.

The Christian woman must approach tasks with the idea that she will be successful in completing the tasks by the grace of God. She knows that it is not she who directs her steps – but it is the Lord. She must not be quick to boast of her accomplishments for she knows that in doing so she is taking the glory from the Lord. She acknowledges that it is by the power and grace of God that she is successful. The Christian woman references the Lord as the source of her strength. She knows that without God she can do nothing but with God she can do all things.

Thought Questions:

1. Have you ever talked with someone who was always bragging?
2. Do you know individuals who feel that they are very, very "important"?
3. What kind of spirit would Christ want us to possess?

Faith and the Wise Christian Woman

Hebrews 11:1 — "Now faith is the substance of things hoped for, the evidence of things not seen."

Emphasizing the necessity of reliance on the belief and assurance that something will occur or come into being although there is no physical evidence of its possible existence captures the essence of faith. Faith lies outside the realm of information which is available to us through our five senses. It evolves around a higher and nobler premise which is the Supremeness of God and the trust that HE will provide for our needs.

Faith allows the Christian woman to take action based on the belief that God will supply her needs. It causes her to do works, having the belief that the end results will be favorable. Faith provides security that if she does according to God's will, those things which are expected to happen will in fact happen. This is called action oriented faith because action is taken based on the belief that God will supply her needs.

Faith allows us to ask of the Father, knowing that we will receive. It causes us to rely not on our own power but the power of God to order our lives and control our being. Faith further underscores the fact the God is "the potter" and "we are the clay."

Faith encompasses hope and expands upon that concept. It is entrenched in the principle that God is able to provide

31

where man can see no means for the provision. It further illustrates the finiteness of man and the infinity of God.

The wise Christian woman knows that faith encourages us to hold on and continue when all signs indicate there is no earthly means for a situation to be altered. When acknowledging the limitations of earth and the creatures found thereon, one is able to appreciate the omnipotence of God.

If the Christian woman is to please God, she will have action oriented faith in dealing with the problems which she may encounter. She will take action with the belief that whatever she asks in faith, she will receive it. She can rest knowing that for every problem, God has a provision because He is faithful and fulfills His promises.

Thought Questions:

1. Have you ever doubted why you need to be a Christian?
2. What do you do when you become weak in the faith?
3. Do you have friends that you can call who are encouragers?

Six Things...
Yea Seven

An Abomination to the Lord...

Proverbs 6:16-19 —"These six things doth the LORD hate: yea, seven are an abomination to him: a proud look, a lying tongue, and hands that shed innocent blood, an heart that deviseth wicked imaginations, feet that be swift in running to mischief, a false witness that speaketh lies, and he that soweth discord among brethren."

The scripture above references the things that GOD hates. They are an abomination, or disgust him. Those are things that the Christian woman does not want to be found possessing. Each of those has to do with traits that are adverse to being Christlike. Those characteristics run counter to the gifts of the spirit, (love, joy, peace, longsuffering, gentleness, goodness, faith, meekness, and temperance). Persons who exhibit the traits that GOD hates, stand in jeopardy of losing their souls, unless they repent and turn from their wicked ways.

The seven negative traits that are listed in the above referenced scripture characterize those behaviors that are of the devil. Sometimes we see those traits made manifest in various ways: (1) Persons who thrive on acting out of pride soon find that they are destroyed by their own conceit. (2) A person who lies is one that cannot be trusted. Many people have lost their lives because someone lied and would not speak the truth. (3) All too often today we see young people become involved in gangs and in the process shed innocent blood as loyalty to the gang. (4) Jesus told us that "out of the abundance of the heart the mouth speaketh." A heart that is full of deceit and wickedness will think of evil acts to commit and cause harm to others. (5) People who run to see a fight or to become involved in an act of violence demonstrate behavior that is very unbecoming to a Christian. (6) Trying to establish truth through a person who will not be truthful will carry no validity when closely examined. (7) A person who keeps disturbances going between relatives or members of the church is one whose words, actions and motives need close scrutiny and cannot be trusted.

Those behaviors are not Christlike and should not be demonstrated by the Christian woman. People who practice those behaviors are not allowing the Spirit of Christ to reign in their lives.

The scriptures tell us that God hates those behaviors. As Christian women, we should in all of our ways, avoid exemplifying any of those characteristics. We should channel our minds to "think on good things"—meditate on the word, hide it in our hearts and be willing to do a kind deed for our fellow sister.

Thought Questions:

1. How can you teach children to be honest?
2. What can be done to show adults that Christ wants harmony in His church?
3. How can Christians encourage other Christians to demonstrate truth and honesty?

"...A proud look,"

Proverbs 6:17

A close study of the scriptures reveals that God does not want us to be proud or haughty. There are many scriptures that let us know that God wants us to be humble and thankful for our blessings. The word "proud" is addressed in fourteen books of the Bible and the word "pride" is addressed in seventeen books of the Bible. There are many scriptures found in those books that have reference to pride and being proud. In each reference there is a negative connotation given to having pride or being proud. We sometimes use the words without really thinking about what we are saying. However, the scriptures tell us that God will bless those who are not proud and be against those who are proud. As is told to us in James 4:6, "...God resisteth the proud, but giveth grace unto the humble." Again in 1 Peter 5:5 we find, "...for God resisteth the proud and giveth grace to the humble." "Pride goeth before destruction, and an haughty spirit before a fall" (Proverbs 16:18).

If we are God's children then we know that everything we have really belongs to God. We are only being allowed to use it and we must be good stewards of our blessings. We must always remember that it is God who fulfills our needs and it is in recognition of His power and might that we should worship Him; giving Him all of the praise and honor.

When we say that we are proud of some accomplishment, we really are taking credit for something that God has allowed to happen. Proverbs 16:5 tells us "Every one that is proud in heart is an abomination to the LORD..." We should seek to express our happiness regarding an event or accomplishment by using terms that do not suggest that we are "proud" of what has occurred. Rather we should try to use terms that say "I am thankful," "I am truly blessed," "I am very humbled," or other phrases which do not covey an element of pride.

Avoiding use of the phrase "I am so proud" can be challenging. However, by knowing that God does not want us to be proud, we will gradually be able to think of other phrases or expressions to relate our enthusiasm about an event or accomplishment.

Thought Questions:

1. Do you have friends who show pride regarding their accomplishments?
2. Have you ever tried to talk with them regarding presenting a more humble spirit?
3. Do you keep in mind the importance of giving God the glory for the accomplishment that you have been blessed to achieve?

"A lying tongue,"

Proverbs 6:17

One of the seven things that are abominations to God is a lying tongue. The scriptures say that God hates a lying tongue and since we know this, as Christians we should do our best (while praying for strength) to avoid telling lies.

The Christian woman should try to avoid persons who lie because she cannot believe what they say. Generally, a person will lie for one of these reasons: to avoid hurt or harm; to gain something; to cause problems for someone else; or to make himself/herself look better. However, there are some persons who lie for the sake of lying, those people are called habitual liars – they have made a habit of not telling the truth. They will tell a 'lie when the truth is more convenient."

The scriptures tell us about people who lie and the lot that befalls them because of lying. In Acts 5:1-10, the story of Ananias and Sapphira is presented telling what happened to them for lying to the apostles. The passage tells how the couple sold their land and kept back a portion, then lied about the amount they received for selling the property. This is a classic case of "the wages of sin is death." They should have told the truth because they were not lying to the apostles but in fact lying to God. And because of their lies, they fell dead instantly.

We find in the scriptures caution regarding how we

interact with each other. The scriptures give us warning signs, regarding the need to avoid certain kinds of people.

Psalm 1 tells us how we should not walk with those who do not present themselves as godly. Details exacting the end for those who follow God's command and those who do not follow His commandments are made clear in this passage of scripture.

James 3:5-13 says that the tongue is a little member and "full of deadly poison," then continues with the idea that no man can tame the tongue. Psalm 39:1-4 tells us that we should keep our tongue and be mindful when the wicked are present. Remembering this can be the key to keeping down a lot of confusion among families and in congregations.

Thought Questions:

1. Have you ever been lied to and you believed the lie?
2. How did it make you feel when you discovered it was a lie?
3. Have you discussed with your child or grandchild how to deal with liars?

"Hands that shed innocent blood"

Proverbs 6:17

God does not want the innocent to suffer at the hand of the wicked. From the beginning, Satan has tried to plant the seeds of wickedness and sin in the minds of God's creation. Satan entered into the heart of Cain and the first murder was committed. Through jealousy and envy innocent lives are taken by those who want to harm the innocent.

God does not want His children to shed innocent blood. This is an abomination to Him and the scriptures warn us against such practices. The emotion of hate that develops in a person to the extent that he/she would take another person's life should never be allowed to grow in the heart of the Christian. People who do not fill their minds with good thoughts will dwell on evil thoughts. From there strongholds develop and then anything is possible.

Often, however, accidents occur through no purposeful intent of a person. That person who caused the accident was not intentionally devising ways to cause innocent blood to be shed. Children have killed other children accidentally by playing with guns. Therefore, children should never be around guns because children are very inquisitive and guns in the hands of children can wreck many lives. Adults who own guns must be careful and responsible gun owners; keeping all guns out of the reach of children.

Shedding innocent blood causes hurt not only to the victim but to the family members of both the victim and the one committing the crime. Many times families suffer long after the event and often never recover. Those who willingly take the lives of innocent people are being controlled by the evil forces of Satan. Hearts which are receptive to committing such acts of violence are void of the love which God wants His children to possess.

Individuals must refrain from becoming so angry that they are willing to take the life of another person. We must, also, teach our children to deal with conflict in a way that is non-violent so that they will not commit such sinful acts nor possibly become the victims of such acts.

Thought Questions:

1. Have you ever known someone whose life was violently taken?
2. Can you imagine the heartache that the family had to endure?
3. Can you think of ways church members might help to ease the pain?

"A heart that deviseth wicked imaginations,..."

Proverbs 6:18

Often in today's world, we see persons making plans for the destruction of others. God does not want us to plot against one another. He does not want us to plan for the demise of others. There are those who devise ways to entrap persons and wait to see if the person escapes. Some people delight in being deceitful, however, God does not want His children to engage in such practices.

The "wicked imaginations" has reference to plans that are made with malice, hate or envy as a part of the motivation to plan. We know that people are always planning and plotting how they can "trick the system," "get over" and/or "play the game." There are also those who want to make everyone else look bad so that they can look good. The Psalmist prayed regarding those who lay traps for others and wait for their downfall. David asked the Lord to allow the angel to chase those who, for no reason, tried to destroy him. This is found in Psalm 35 along with information as to how one should not rejoice at the evil person's demise but show humility and concern, even for the enemy.

Jesus gives us perfect instructions regarding how we should rejoice when others mistreat us and harass us for HIS sake (Matthew 5:11-12). If we suffer persecution here on earth for HIS sake, we have a reward in heaven.

When people allow their minds to go unchallenged by the Word of God, they are not being bridled in their thinking. Studying the Word allows the mind to concentrate on positive thoughts and guard against "wicked imaginations." Evil enters where there is a lack of spiritual presence. We are cautioned in the scriptures to guard our minds and think on good things (Philippians 4:8).

Some women delight in seeing other women defeated or belittled. They often plot on their jobs to see if they can cause someone to be suspended or fired. Generally, it is because of jealousy. The Christian woman should avoid being taken in by deceit or trickery. Always remember Psalm 1 which gives admonition regarding "walketh not in the counsel of the ungodly." The Christian woman who meditates on the Word of God will not be overtaken by the evil devices of the wicked.

Thought Questions:

1. Have you ever met a person who only thought about what" she" or "he" wanted?
2. How do you interact with that kind of person?
3. How can you influence that person to become Christlike?

...Feet That Run Swiftly to Mischief

Proverbs 6:18

Generally, when we hear the word "mischief" we may think of an innocent prank or trick that someone has done. We may think about some playful manner that people use in order to side-step doing the right thing as being mischievous. However, when reading descriptions of mischief in the Bible, we come away with a more serious thought about mischief.

Each reference that is made to "mischief" in the Bible has a very negative meaning. As spoken of in the Bible, mischief has to do with deceit, conniving and basic evil being done by someone to someone else. The reference in Proverbs 6:18 connects mischief to one of the seven acts that God hates. Those who run to mischief or the feet that run "swiftly" to mischief are included as one of the acts that greatly displeases God.

Have you ever seen children run to where they think a fight is about to take place, or who make plans to be at a certain place to witness an argument that they heard was about to happen? We, as Christian women, need to discourage our children and/or relatives from running to a fight or an argument. Often times an innocent by-stander can become a victim by being in the wrong place at the wrong time. We should encourage our young people to leave places that are known for fights, and they should never run to see a fight. When two people are going to fight, if they have an audience, the fight will more than likely happen. If there is no audience, often the persons will not fight.

People who go places with evil intent in their hearts have feet that run swiftly to mischief. It is considered as mischief when a person goes out of his/her way to do evil to someone. Learning to avoid those situations is something that should be stressed. As Christian women, we are to teach others the way of Christ. Older women are to teach the younger women and we teach best by example. We should refrain from becoming involved in acts that are deceitful, evil and/or mischievous.

Thought Questions:

1. Do you find opportunities to talk with young people?
2. Do you try to encourage them in doing good things?
3. Do we as Christians provide enough opportunities for children to fill their leisure time with positive activities?

"A false witness that speaketh lies..."

Proverbs 6:19

It is an abomination to the Lord for someone to be a false witness and speak lies. This is an all inclusive statement because it describes the person who serves as a false witness and details what that false witness does. On our jobs, we may see people conspiring with one another to lie about a coworker, having it supported by someone who serves as a witness and knowingly lies about the other person. People have lost their jobs, their homes, their marriages, and yes, even their lives because of a false witness.

In reading the accounts of what happened to Jesus, we know that there were those who came to bear false witness against Him, but their testimony was not accepted because they could not agree (Mark 14:55-59). We should know that if the people lied about Jesus, they will lie about us. To agree to do wrong and testify to an event that one knows did not happen, is willful lying. Some people, however, do not have problems serving as a witness to a lie, even when they are well aware that what they are saying is not true. A false witness is one who lies knowingly and is a dangerous individual who stands in danger of the second death (Revelations 21:8).

Many times people cannot stand up to peer pressure. Even some adults fall victim to peer pressure in an effort to be "accepted" and "fit in." Working in concert to lie about another person is wrong. Those who lie about others cannot be trusted and often will turn on the one that has been a part of the lie. There is no honor among liars and we know that the devil "is a liar, and the father of it" (John 8:44).

As Christian women we should avoid persons who serve as witnesses for lies against others. We should encourage our children, grandchildren and other relatives to avoid persons who willfully lie and who try to entrap others.

Thought Questions:

1. Have you ever listened as someone lied and then heard someone else serve as a witness to the lie?
2. How do you deal with a false witness?
3. How can you be a positive influence in such situations?

"...He that soweth discord among brethren."

Proverbs 6:19

The last behavior identified as one of the seven things that are abominations to God is "he that soweth discord among brethren." This abomination has a far reaching impact upon the church. The term "brethren" is inclusive of all persons that are members of the church. God hates it when Christians go about causing unrest, strife and discord among members of the body of Christ.

Paul, in his epistles to the church at Corinth, was very strong in his warnings to persons who cause strife in the church. The first epistle to the Corinthians reveals that there was much unrest among the members of the body at that location. The warnings that Paul gave to them are applicable to us today. As Christians, we should not be caught up with envying our fellow sisters, or causing dissentions among members. In 1 Corinthians 1:11 Paul writes, "For it hath been declared unto me of you, my brethren, by them which are of the house of Chloe, that there are contentions among you." We should not be walking like the Corinthians, but walk in the Spirit and not in the flesh. When we were baptized, we put on the new person and are to be focusing on things that will help us on our journey from earth to glory.

John, also, writes regarding persons who sowed discord in the church. In 3 John verse 9 we read about Diotrephes and how he loved to be above others in the church. He was arrogant and would not receive his fellow Christians. Diotrephes even went so far as to try to put people out of the church. Diotrephes was a sower of discord and caused many problems in the early church.

As Christian women, we should not be involved in talking negatively about our fellow sisters. We are not to be a party to arguments, disputes and backbiting. In Paul's letter to the church at Philippi he tells them "do all things without murmurings and disputing" (Philippians 2:14). Christians are to be a light in a world of darkness. Our light must shine to the glory of Christ for others to know that we are members of His body (Matthew 5:16). Christian women should not be a part of cliques that go about causing dissentions among sisters. Our work on earth (living the life that will lead souls to Christ) is too important for us to become involved with situations that cause us to be unkind to one another. Rather than tearing each other down we should be building each other up. "Let nothing be done through strife and vainglory; but in lowliness of mind let each esteem other better than themselves" (Philippians 2:3).

Thought Questions:

1. Do you know sisters who delight when there is friction among other sisters?
2. Have you observed instances where cliques operate within the church and keep confusion brewing?
3. How can you serve as a catalyst to stop negative talk and behavior among sisters?

God's Seasons

God and Seasons

Ecclesiastes 3:1 — "To every thing there is a season..."

This passage in Ecclesiastes which deals with "seasons" has to do with the times in our lives. The writer is clear that the various events which happen in our lives are there only for a while and then other occurrences take place. Man is bound by time, from birth until death. Events on man's calendar are all measured by time. Time is fleeting and is in constant motion. The phrase time waits for no one is true because each second represents another aspect of time.

We, as humans, often want time to roll back and have situations to be as they once were in our lives. This can never happen, but God has blessed us with memories by which we can recall events. God already knows the future for each person because He knows what decisions we will make and what actions we will take. God allows us to be free moral agents and by the decisions that we make, we determine whether our destiny will be eternity with Him or eternity with the devil. Anything that happens on this earth was known already by God from the beginning of time. Because God is infinite, the Creator of time and the One who will determine when time shall be no more, He moves in His own time (Revelations 10:6).

The passage cited from Ecclesiastes helps us to understand that there is a time for everything to happen and events happen in their own time. The seasons of the year are not determined by man but by God. The rain, wind, sunlight and darkness are all determined by God. Often the tragedies and unpleasant circumstances that come in our lives are there for us to grow, and develop , and are there for only a short time. Man's very life is only for "a little time, and then vanisheth away" (James 4:14).

We can do nothing to interfere with the seasons and natural elements that God has ordained. Nothing happens on earth without God's knowledge. God determines when the soul is released from the body. Although outside forces may place a person in a position to die, only God requires the soul to leave the body. We need to learn to enjoy the minute, or endure the pain because there is comfort in knowing that it is only for a season.

The scriptures tell us that in everything we should give thanks. We should praise God in every situation that we find ourselves knowing that "all things work together for good to them that love God, to them who are the called according to his purpose" (Romans 8:28).

God is Omnipresent, Omnipotent and Omniscient. A thousand years is but one day in the sight of God, for time is of no consequence to God (2 Peter 3:8). God is the Sender of the second, the Maker of the moment, the Holder of the hour, the Deliverer of the day, the Wielder of the week, the Master of the month, and the Yahweh of the year.

Thought Questions:

1. Have you ever wished that you could go back to the way things use to be?
2. Have you considered the positives and the negatives of "going back"?
3. Do you talk with young people about how the decisions that they make now may impact them for the rest of their lives?

In God's Time

Ephesians 1:10—"That in the dispensation of the fullness of times..."

God's time is "perfect" time and man can do nothing to improve upon it. God, in His own time, moves and causes things to happen. His timing is not our timing and we must learn to be in keeping with His time. How do we do that? We must "inquire of the Lord." We must pray to the Lord and wait until He decides whether He will grant our request or cause us to wait until a more appropriate "season." Often our requests are not granted because we are not at a point in our lives when we should receive the requests. God knows when events should occur and at His appointed time they will occur.

We may be too "full of ourselves" at the time of the request. God may have to "empty us out" before He can "fill us up." We may have to lose the pride and self-conceit before He will bless us. Often we stand in the way of our own blessings. Many times we don't want to give a blessing to others (doing something for someone else) because we want someone to do something for us. It may be that a person has to forget self, and serve others. The time may not be right for our blessing but it may be time for us to bless others.

When we study our Bibles, we read about the tribulations of Job. We know that he was tried by the devil, and suffered much pain as a result. Yet through all of his misery, he resolved "all the days of my appointed time will I wait, till my change come" (Job 14:14). When we find ourselves overwhelmed with problems, sickness and unrest, we must resolve to wait for our change.

Though times may be troubled, problems many, patience short and finances low, do not become dismayed or depressed because in God's time, He will bring you through the storms. Remember the scripture "We are troubled on every side, yet not distressed; we are perplexed, but not in despair; persecuted, but not forsaken; cast down, but not destroyed" (2 Corinthians 4:8-9). As Christian women, we know that "time is an agent of the future" and God holds the future. We must have faith in God that in due time He will change our circumstances and be comforted in the knowledge that He "ever cares and provides for his own." In time, we will look back and say "and it came to pass" because "time brings about a change."

Thought Questions:

1. Are you content during this season in which you find yourself?
2. Have you taken time to encourage someone who may be having difficulties?
3. Do you know of any times in your life when God has intervened just at the moment you needed Him most?

The Power of Words

Words Have Power

Psalm 141:3 — "Set a watch, O LORD, before my mouth; keep the door of my lips."

Words are powerful and they can have lasting effects upon persons who hear the words. Some adults can never see themselves as successful because of negative words that were spoken to them when they were children. Words are so powerful that the Psalmist asked the Lord to keep watch over the "door of my lips" so that only good things could come from his lips. We are encouraged in Paul's letter to the Ephesians to "Let no corrupt communication proceed out of your mouth, but that which is good to the use of edifying, that it may minister grace unto the hearers"(Ephesians 4:29). We find here that words can minister to the needs of those who hear the words. In this case words are used to build up a person and cause one to feel good. In like manner, words can serve to tear people down and cause them to feel badly about themselves and others. We must be careful how we use words.

There are people who delight in speaking evil, or demeaning words to others. These people use their tongues as weapons upon defenseless victims. Some are very crafty with speaking evil, and their words can penetrate so deeply it takes years to overcome their impact. We need to "taste" our words before we utter them. Solomon, the wisest man that ever lived, said in Ecclesiastes 5:2, "Be not rash with thy mouth and let not thine heart be hasty to utter any thing before God...." Everything we say is heard by God.

As Christians, we need to try to build each other up and refrain from speaking evil of each other. We should discourage others from talking about people and not let evil come from our lips. Jesus said "There is nothing from without a man, that entering into him can defile him: but the things which come out of him, those are they that defile the man" (Mark 7:15). What we say to others can cause them to stop trying, accept defeat and never accomplish the goals that are before them. Negative words can take hold over a person's mind and cause that person to become depressed and apathetic.

Care should be taken in uttering words because once we have said them, we can never take them back. Words are powerful and God used words to speak this world into existence. We edify and we mortify with words. We need to be thoughtful in speaking and exercise wisdom in our conversations.

Thought Questions:

1. Have you used words to change the way people view situations?
2. Have you ever observed the influence words have on a person's attitude?
3. How can we use words to build self-confidence of others?

Speaking Words of Encouragement

Proverbs 25:11 — "A word fitly spoken is like apples of gold in pictures of silver."

As we travel "life's railway to heaven," we will face many obstacles and many disappointments. Those obstacles and disappointments should not cause the Christian woman to become discouraged in her walk with the Lord. It is through hardships that we develop courage, character and faith. Fellow sisters can provide that much needed assurance to the one who is cast down and burdened with problems and worries. Often a word of encouragement, reassuring statements regarding how God loves her, reminders of the promises of God, and statements of declaration as to God's faithfulness, can be the sources of encouragement that a fellow sister needs.

Many times a sister can feel rejected, disheartened and depressed, needing an uplifting word to help focus on the positive aspects of life. The Lord may send you to that person at the right time to speak the right words which will bring that person out of the state of depression. Kind words to one who is depressed is like the "fresh rain on a dying flower."

As Christian women, we need to be encouragers and uplifters. Encouragers allow persons to get that second wind that is so needed in order to continue to tread up the hills of challenge and through the valleys of despair while journeying from earth to glory. Encouraging others in the faith will help them see that every problem, every trouble, every obstacle is an opportunity for reliance on the Lord. Faith is strengthened through hard times, and reaching out to God is enhanced during our hours of despair. The Lord wants us to give Him our burdens which will ease our traveling load (Matthew 11:28-30).

Individuals who can find positive things to say in very negative situations, have a gift that should be shared with others. People need reinforcement of the positive aspects of life and should be encouraged to pursue those plans which will be beneficial to them.

We should seek to bring words of encouragement which will help to lighten the burden a sister may be carrying. Just to know that someone cares enough to speak a kind word can bring light into a room of darkness.

Thought Questions:

1. Have you seized the opportunity today to encourage someone?
2. Do you find it hard to give words of encouragement to others?
3. What words of encouragement would you have for someone who just lost a loved one?

Let the Redeemed Say So

Psalm 107:2 — "Let the redeemed of the LORD say so, whom he hath redeemed from the hand of the enemy."

We, who have been redeemed by the blood of the Lamb should be so excited about that redemption that we share the good news of our salvation at each opportunity. There should be joy and excitement because we have been washed in the blood of the Lamb and we are now in position to inherit eternal life. We "say so" by the words we speak and the behavior we demonstrate.

Often we do not realize that people are observing us in various situations. Many times the life that we live before others will say whether we are redeemed or not. We say we are redeemed by the company that we keep, by the places that we go and by the manner of our conversation. The redeemed of the Lord are those who exemplify the Spirit of the Lord. The words that we utter and the manner in which we present ourselves, in large measure will send the message of our redemption. There should be a presence that the Christian woman has when interacting with others that will signal there is something different about her. When asked about this "difference" the Christian should be willing to share the "hope that lies within" her. This hope is the living hope which is based on the redemption that has been received as a result of obedience to Christ.

Some people may never read an epistle of the Bible, nor attend a church gathering, but they may have contact with those who profess Christianity. That association could determine if those people will ever come to the knowledge of the Lord. They read the epistles of our lives and how we conduct ourselves. While working on our jobs, or interacting with others in various settings, situations may arise that will be prime opportunities to demonstrate the life of a redeemed saint. When the Christian is falsely accused, or mistreated by a coworker, how that individual handles the situation may influence positively or negatively those who are watching. When in difficult situations we truly let others know that we are redeemed, if our actions "say so."

Thought Questions:

1. Have you had an opportunity to share Jesus with someone who is not saved?
2. Have you ever felt that someone was "setting you up" to see if they could cause you to act in a way that was not Christlike?
3. Does your behavior at work reflect that you are a Christian?

CPSIA information can be obtained at www.ICGtesting.com
Printed in the USA
LVOW13s0747081213

364375LV00001B/2/P